DISCARD

Fact Finders®

The Story of Sanitation

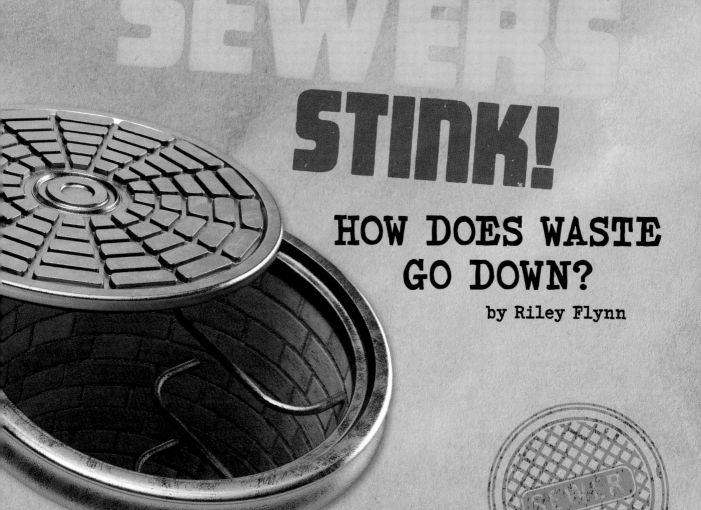

SEWERS STINK!

HOW DOES WASTE GO DOWN?

by Riley Flynn

SEWER

CAPSTONE PRESS
a capstone imprint

Fact Finder Books are published by Capstone Press,
1710 Roe Crest Drive, North Mankato, Minnesota 56003
www.mycapstone.com

Library of Congress Cataloging-in-Publication Data
Library of Congress Cataloging-in-Publication data is available on the Library of Congress website.

ISBN 978-1-5435-3113-8 (hardback)
ISBN 978-1-5435-3117-6 (paperback)
ISBN 978-1-5435-3121-3 (eBook PDF)

Editorial Credits
Anna Butzer, editor; Bobbie Nuytten, designer;
Morgan Walters, media researcher; Kris Wilfahrt, production specialist

Photo Credits
Alamy: ART Collection, 10, top 28; Getty Images: sola deo gloria, 9; iStockphoto: BlackJack3D,
27; Shutterstock: Abel Feyman, 8, Aleks Melnik, Cover, Alon Othnay, Cover, AuntSpray, 15,
Avatar_023, 17, Dimitar Sotirov, Cover, djmilic, 1, focal point, 26, I WALL, (paper) design element
throughout, karamysh, 5, Kekyalyaynen, 20, Lyudvig Aristarhovich, 19, Mei Yi, bottom left
14, bottom middle 14, bottom right 14, michaelheim, 23, 29, Milosz_G, 13, Nomad_Soul, 11,
Rawpixel.com, 25, Renata Sedmakova, 22, saknakorn, 4, bottom 28, stockphoto-graf, 24, tele52,
18, Thuwanan Krueabudda, 21, Toa55, 16, Vladimir Mulder, 6, Wanna Thongpao, 7, Zurijeta, 12

Printed and bound in the United States.
PA021

TABLE OF CONTENTS

CHAPTER 1
A SEWER RUNS THROUGH IT

The commode, porcelain throne, powder room, stool pool, or loo. No matter what you call it, it's the place to go when you need relief. Everybody does their business—numbers one and two—but not everyone knows what happens after they flush. Most of us don't think twice about what goes down the toilet . . . as long as it doesn't come back up.

Toilets use different amounts of water to flush. Some older versions can use up to 7 gallons (26 liters) per flush!

Flushable toilets help keep our homes and cities clean. Sinks are great for washing hands and dishes. Showers give us privacy when it is time to rinse off. But have you ever wondered what happens after the water we use goes down the drain? Have you ever wondered where all that stuff goes? No? Well it's time to find out!

Help conserve water by taking showers instead of baths. Keep your shower short to save more water.

What Is Wastewater?

   Did you know that anything that goes down
a drain is classified as sewage? Another term for
sewage is wastewater. Wastewater is any water that
has been used by humans. Wastewater often contains
feces (poop), urine (pee), and cleaning chemicals.
In the United States, the average person produces
nearly 100 gallons (379 liters) of wastewater per day.
That's a lot of dirty water! That's why sewers and
wastewater treatment centers are so important.

Sewer inspectors
have the nasty job of
examining sewer lines.

Treatment plants reduce **pollutants** in wastewater to a level nature can handle.

We live on a planet that is 70 percent water. But only a small percentage of it is available for humans to use. There is not enough water on the planet for all the people living here. That's why it's important that wastewater goes through a recycling process at treatment facilities. Sewers are a huge part of the process that wastewater has to go through.

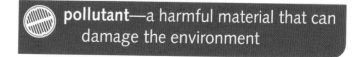

pollutant—a harmful material that can damage the environment

CHAPTER 2

PLUMBING THROUGH THE AGES

Imagine what your city would be like if sewer systems didn't exist. Wastewater would flow through the streets, and an awful smell would constantly fill the air. Every now and then, it would rain, and the waste and its smelly odor would be washed away. But wait! That waste, *human* waste, would just be washed into nearby rivers or lakes. Unfortunately, before sewer systems were created in the late 1800s, that's how people in Europe and the United States lived.

Ancient Plumbing

The Indus people lived 4,000 years ago in what is now Pakistan. They had a system of street drains and indoor toilets. The Indus poured water down the drains which pushed waste into a system of brick pipes. The Indus wisely directed these pipes away from their sources of drinking water. This system kept people from getting sick.

FACT The first sewer system in America was built in 1842 in Mohawk, New York.

The ancient Romans built an early version of public restrooms.

Pots and Pits

Unfortunately, later civilizations didn't continue using the plumbing methods created by the Indus people. Instead of toilets, people used **chamber pots**. Cities didn't have pipes to take waste away, so people had **cesspools** in their basements or backyards. A cesspool is a hole where human waste, rotting food, and other garbage are thrown.

Some people emptied their chamber pots in the streets or in nearby water sources.

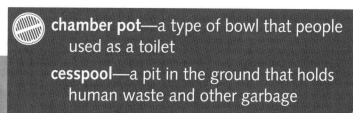

chamber pot—a type of bowl that people used as a toilet

cesspool—a pit in the ground that holds human waste and other garbage

9

Filthy Cities and First Flushes

John Harrington invented the first water closet in 1596. It was an early version of the flushable toilet we know and love today. More than 200 years passed before Harrington's idea caught on because most people saw no reason to install toilets. To them, it was easier to dump a chamber pot out the window. At that time, there were no sewer systems so there was nowhere for the waste to go. Without sewers, waste ended up outside one way or another.

John Harrington
(1561–1612)

But as the population grew in Europe and the United States, so did the number of cesspools. The smell of human waste hung in the air. And the germs from the waste eventually polluted the drinking water. Terrible diseases killed thousands of people. It was time to do something to keep waste off the streets and keep the waterways clean. People needed sewers. By the late 1800s, many large U.S. cities had them.

SAVED BY SEWERS

In the 1500s many Europeans developed a fear of bathing. They believed that if they got wet they would become sick. No one knew that it was really the germs and bacteria in the water that was making them sick. Today we know that illnesses can be spread through human waste and dirty water. This makes us even more grateful for our sewer systems.

CHAPTER 3

FROM FLUSH TO FINISH

Think about all the times you've flushed the toilet, done the dishes, brushed your teeth, or taken a shower. Where does all that used water go? Wastewater doesn't just disappear after it goes down the drain. Today many people's toilets, sinks, showers, and other water fixtures in their homes are all connected.

Scrape any leftover food into the trash before doing dishes. Food scraps can clog up pipes fast and cause a big problem.

If you go into the basement of your home, you'll probably see a tall pipe about 6 inches (15 centimeters) around. It's connected to your toilet. Plumbers call it the stack. The stack takes waste to the sewer line.

The sewer line leads wastewater to pipes under the street. Sewer lines flow downward from small pipes to bigger pipes. Each pipe goes lower and lower into the ground.

Some wastewater pipes can be easily seen. Others are hidden behind walls.

Journey Through the Pipes

Eventually all pipes connect to the main sewer line. This is a large pipe deep underground. Some main sewer lines are large enough for an adult to stand up in. Even bigger main sewer lines have a wide stream in the middle and walkways on each side. The water flowing in the main sewer line holds all the wastewater from every sink, toilet, and tub in the area. That gunky water makes its way to a sewage treatment plant.

UNDERGROUND ACCESS

Manhole covers are an important piece to the sewer system. These round plates provide access to the pipes underneath our cities. Thanks to manholes, maintenance workers can easily climb down into the sewers to fix any problems. There are about 20 million manhole covers in the United States. Some countries decorate their manhole covers with designs. Pretty and practical!

SANITARY SEWER SYSTEM

sanitary manhole

after the flush

to sewage treatment plant

sewage flow direction

What Happens at the Sewage Treatment Plant?

What happens to that gigantic underground stream of water, bodily waste, and other nasty stuff? Before the late 1800s, that wastewater was dumped directly back into rivers. Eventually people realized that dirty water was making them sick and that wastewater needed to be cleaned. Today wastewater is cleaned at treatment plants.

FACT Wastewater treatment centers in the United States process about 34 billion gallons (129 billion liters) of wastewater every day.

Wastewater treatment plants help keep dirty water like this out of our lakes and rivers.

At the Treatment Plant

At treatment plants, wastewater goes through five major stages: screening, primary treatment, secondary treatment, **disinfection**, and sludge treatment. Before wastewater can be treated, the solid objects that found their way into the sewer need to be removed. During the screening process, special screens trap large pieces of trash, sticks, newspapers, bottles, face wipes, diapers, and more. This garbage is taken away to landfills.

Watewater treatment plant workers make sure that the wastewater is being cleaned properly.

disinfect—to use chemicals to kill germs

Primary Treatment

After the solids are strained from the wastewater, it is still filled with human waste, poisonous gases, and germs. These things pollute rivers and can harm people and animals. The wastewater is moved to **sedimentation** tanks. Any solids still in the wastewater sink to the bottom of the tanks. These solids are called sludge. The sludge is pumped away for further treatment, and the wastewater is moved to large tanks for secondary treatment.

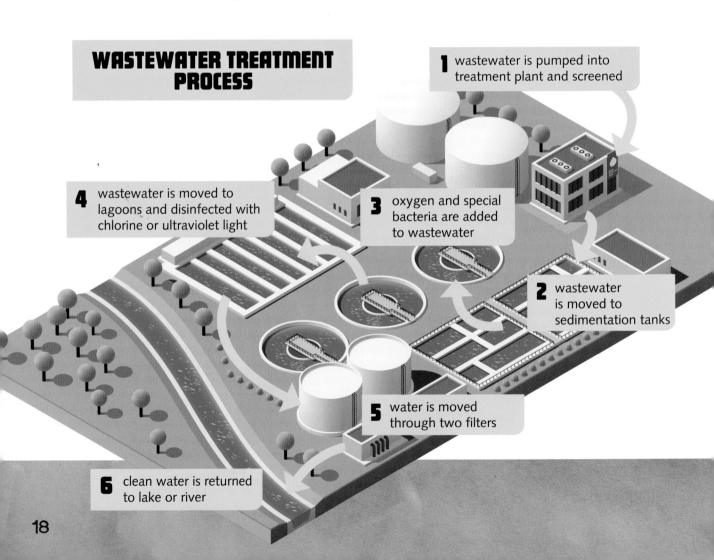

WASTEWATER TREATMENT PROCESS

1 wastewater is pumped into treatment plant and screened

4 wastewater is moved to lagoons and disinfected with chlorine or ultraviolet light

3 oxygen and special bacteria are added to wastewater

2 wastewater is moved to sedimentation tanks

5 water is moved through two filters

6 clean water is returned to lake or river

Secondary Treatment

Wastewater is moved to large tanks where workers add oxygen and special bacteria to it. This is called secondary treatment. Oxygen makes the bacteria grow quickly. As the bacteria grow, they eat the pollutants in the water. When the bacteria run out of food, they die. The water left behind is a lot cleaner than it was before, but the wastewater still passes through two more **filters**. One uses sand, and the other uses charcoal. These filters help remove any remaining germs.

FACT Primary and secondary treatments remove about 85 to 95 percent of pollutants before the treated wastewater is disinfected.

 sedimentation—a process that cleans water by allowing small particles to sink to the bottom and be removed

filter—a device that cleans liquids or gases as they pass through it

Look at the bubbles on top of the wastewater in the tank. That is what happens when oxygen is added to it.

Disinfection

Finally, the wastewater begins a process called **lagooning**, where it is pumped into large ponds. Any remaining solid waste settles to the bottom, leaving clean water on the top. Many cities grow plants in the lagoons because plants eat even more bad bacteria.

a wastewater treatment plant

lagooning—a process during which wastewater sits in artificial ponds, allowing solid waste to sink to the bottom

As the wastewater is pumped into these ponds, it is disinfected. Some cities use chlorine, the same chemical that cleans swimming pools. However, many animals drink treated water once it is released back into lakes and rivers. Unfortunately, studies have shown that chlorine causes cancer in some animals. Because of this, many cities now use ultraviolet light to disinfect water.

Water is exposed to ultraviolet light in a water treatment pond.

Sludge Treatment

After the sludge and wastewater have been separated, the sludge is moved from storage tanks to a **dewatering** center. There, sludge is moved to a large, rotating machine called a centrifuge. The centrifuge acts similar to the spin cycle of a washing machine. The **centrifugal force** from spinning fast separates the rest of the water from the sludge.

dewatering—the removal of water from solid material

centrifugal force—the physical force that causes a body rotating around a center to move away from the center

Some treatment plants don't have dewatering machines. At those plants the sludge is moved through a pipeline, or by a sludge boat, to a plant with a dewatering machine.

Some treated wastewater can be used to make energy. It can also be recycled to make water that can be used on farms. Some countries, including Australia and Singapore, make recycled drinking water out of treated sewage.

CHAPTER 4

HOW OUR WASTEWATER AFFECTS OUR WORLD

Wastewater needs to be properly treated before it can be disposed of. If it's not, it can **contaminate** water and harm plants and animals in rivers or oceans.

contaminate—to make dirty or unfit for use

Sewage that has been properly treated can still cause problems. Researchers have found that microscopic plastic fibers can make it through the wastewater treatment plants. These particles have been found in fish and shellfish that humans eat. They have also been found in our tap water. Researchers believe these small plastic fibers come from washing clothes made from synthetic fabrics.

Buying clothing with natural fibers instead of synthetic can help reduce the amount of plastic in our water.

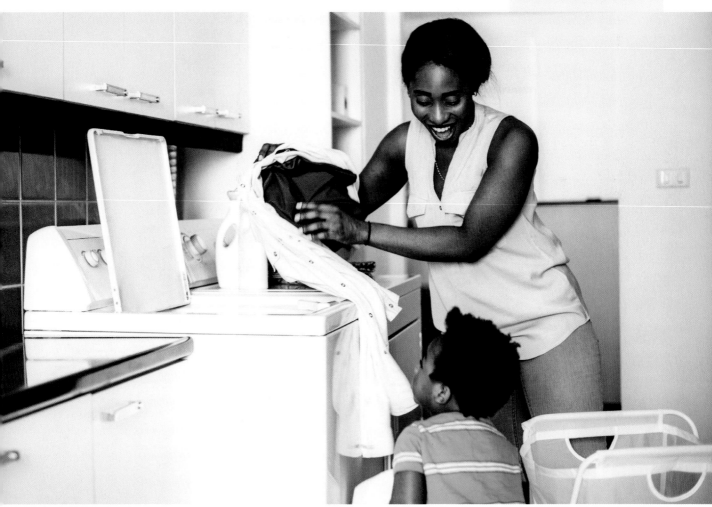

Make a Difference

The way we treat sewage now is a lot better than in the past. But billions of gallons of partially treated sewage still make it into our lakes and rivers every year. Even sewage that hasn't been treated can sometimes get into our water sources. This can be caused by sewer overflows or leaking pipes.

With the shortage of clean water, it is important that we do all we can to help keep water safe. It is everyone's responsibility to make sure household products are thrown away correctly.

Sewers make our world a much cleaner place to live, and it is our job to help keep them working properly.

FACT Cleaning products with hazardous chemicals should never be poured down a drain. These toxins could end up polluting a river, lake, or stream.

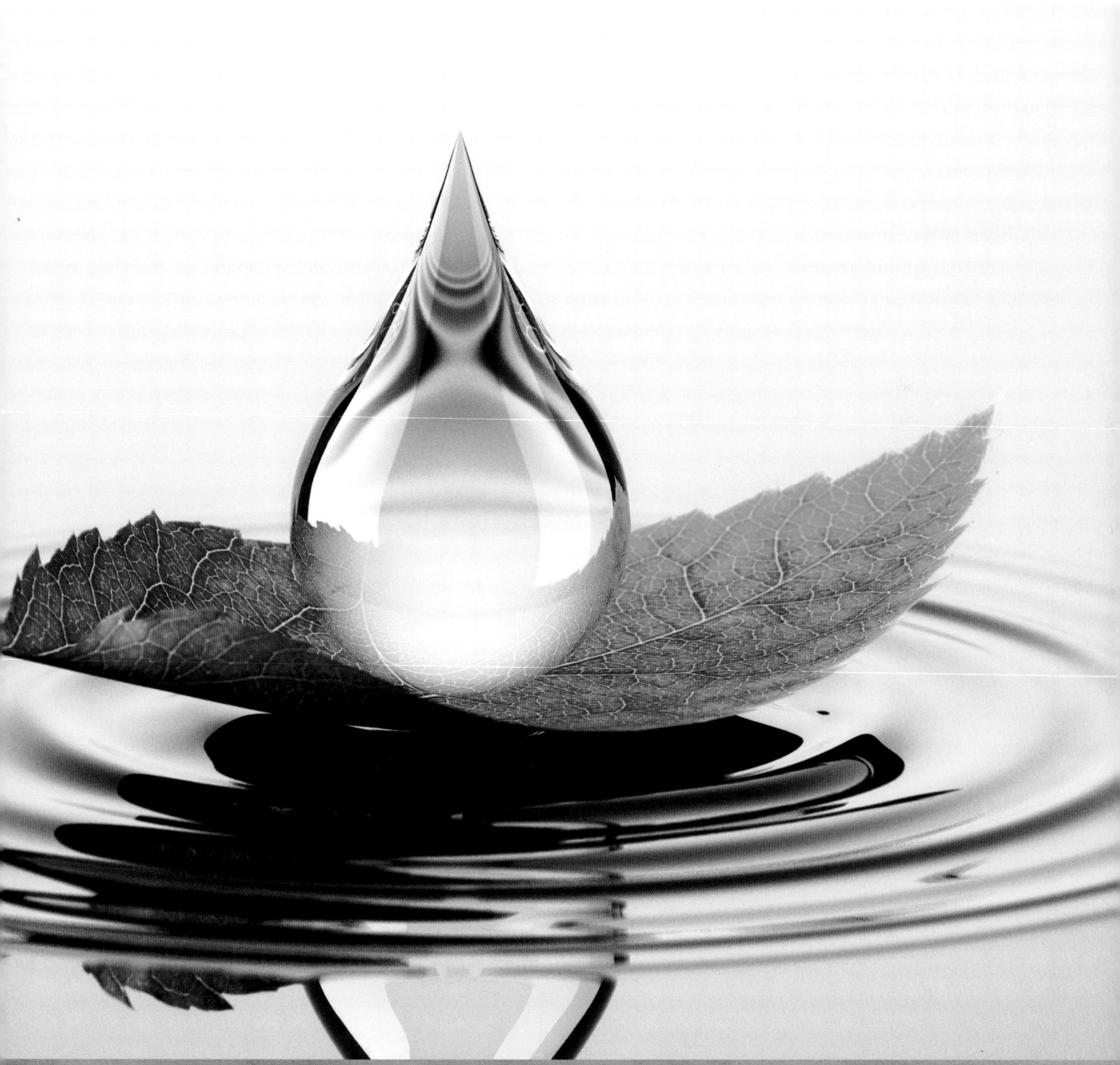

TIMELINE

500 BC
Underground sewers were built in ancient Rome.

1388
England outlaws dumping of waste in streets and public waterways.

1596
John Harrington designed the first flushing toilet for his godmother, Queen Elizabeth I. It released waste into a cesspool.

1851
The flush toilet is first introduced to the public.

1855
The first sewer systems in the United States are built in New York and Illinois.

500 BC   1400   1800

1981

The International Drinking Water Supply and Sanitatation Decade is launched to support clean water and sanitation worldwide.

1883

The first septic tank is introduced in the United States.

1923

The world's first large-scale sludge plant is built in Wisconsin.

1985

The Great Pacific Garbage Patch is discovered in the Pacific Ocean. Large amounts of plastic, chemical sludge, and other debris are pushed together by ocean movement.

1900

1990

GLOSSARY

centrifugal force (sen-TRI-fyuh-guhl FORS)—the physical force that causes a body rotating around a center to move away from the center

cesspool (SESS-pool)—a pit in the ground that holds human waste and other garbage

chamber pot (CHAYM-buhr POT)—a type of bowl that people used as a toilet

contaminate (kuhn-TA-muh-nayt)—to make dirty or unfit for use

dewatering (di-waw-ter-ing)—the removal of water from solid material

disinfect (dis-in-FEKT)—to use chemicals to kill germs

filter (FIL-tuhr)—a device that cleans liquids or gases as they pass through it; water can be cleaned by going through a filter made of sand, gravel, or charcoal

lagooning (luh-GOON-ing)—a process during which wastewater sits in artificial ponds, allowing solid waste to sink to the bottom

pollutant (puh-LOOT-uhnt)—a harmful material that can damage the environment

sedimentation (sed-uh-muhn-TAY-shun)—a process that cleans water by allowing small particles to sink to the bottom and be removed

READ MORE

Canavan, Roger. *You Wouldn't Want to Live Without Clean Water!* You Wouldn't Want To. New York: Franklin Watts, 2015.

Feinstein, Stephen. *Drying Up: Running Out of Water.* The End of Life as We Know It. New York: Enslow Publishing, 2016.

Olien, Rebecca. *Cleaning Water.* Water In Our World. North Mankato, Minn.: Capstone Press, 2016.

INTERNET SITES

FactHound offers a safe, fun way to find Internet sites related to this book. All of the sites on FactHound have been researched by our staff.

Here's all you do:

Visit *www.facthound.com*

Type in this code: 9781543531138

Check out projects, games and lots more at
www.capstonekids.com

CRITICAL THINKING QUESTIONS

1. What would our world be like without wastewater treatment plants? How would life be different?

2. What are some ways you can help keep our sewers working properly and keep our water sources clean?

3. How much wastewater does an average person produce in a day? What are some ways we can cut back on water usage?

INDEX